LITTLE MISS,

Wash Your

HANDS!

Publisher: That's Love Publishing LLC
Printed in the United States of America.
ISBN 978-1-953751-05-8

First printing, 2021.
Orders by U.S. trade bookstores and wholesalers
Please contact E.Basora
at thatslovepublishing@gmail.com
Website: thatslovepublishing.com

Dedication

This book is dedicated to all the littles I have ever taught. To all the OR staff who have heard me say "Gel in and Gel out" and know the art of hand washing is the first line of defense against surgical site infections. To my own littles, I love you.

Little Miss it is time to eat!
You better move those feet!

Hey Little Miss come give me a kiss
But do not touch this and this and this.
Be on the way to wash those hands,
No arguing with me, the order stands.

Not sure why, I was just playing outside.
But I do as I am told
So, I do not get a scold.

I run to the kitchen sink, but cannot reach.
So, Mama brings a stool to be a peach.
"Hey, Little Miss! Do I need to help you
with this?" "I think I got this," as I pretend
to grab soap from the dish.

Mama spies my trick and gives me the eye,
I smile back at Mama just as sweet as pie.
Soap is what I know I need,
But I really just want to eat some beans.

Little Miss, I think you missed the soap.
I grab the soap, wash my palms, and hope.
I count ONE, TWO, THREE.
I am done and run the water until
the soap is all free.

Hey, Little Miss you forgot to wash your fingers,
Are you sure you don't want me to linger?
I can help you properly wash those hands,
So, you are clean and germ free from all
those hand stands.

Ok Mama can you help me with this? This time, Mama gets her wish, As I ask for her help with this.

Yes, my love, washing your hands is even more important right now. Let me stand next to you and show you how:

Step 1: Get your singing voice warmed up "La, La, La."

Step 2: Turn the water on, rinse your hands, and start singing the Happy Birthday song.

Step 3: Rub soap on the front and back of your hands and keep singing your song.

Step 4: Wash in between and all around each of your 10 fingers—start with your thumb.

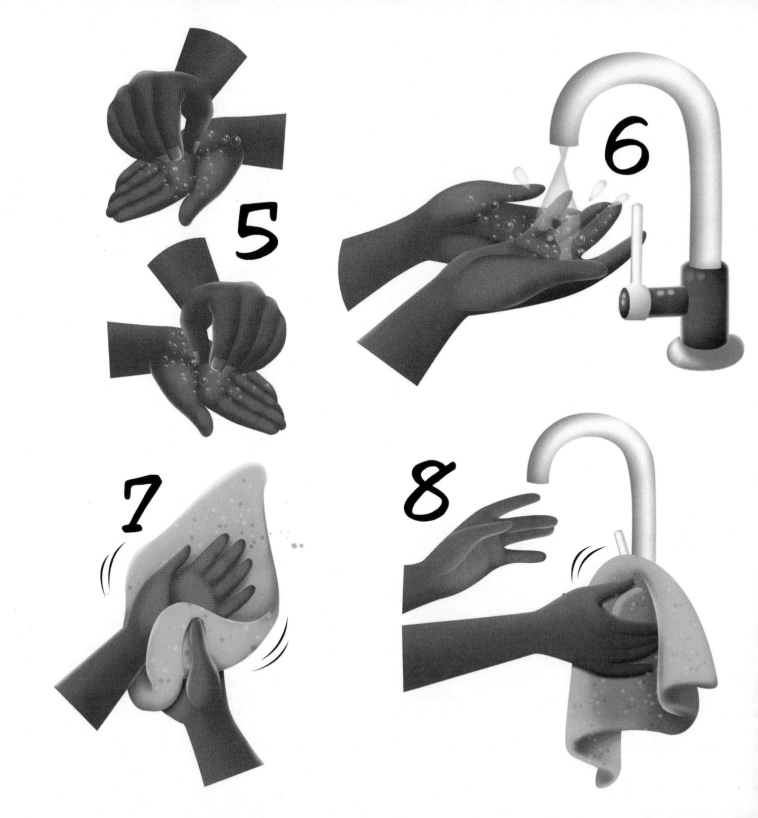

Step 5: Be sure to get underneath your fingernails while finishing up your song.

Step 6: Rinse all the soap off your hands with water.

Step 7: Dry your hands with a towel.

Step 8: Use that towel to turn off the faucet.

Once Mama shows me how,
I am ready to try it on my own right
now! I warm up my singing voice and jump
right into step 2:
Step 2: Turn the water on, rinse your
            hands, and start singing the
            Happy Birthday song.
Step 3: Rub soap on the front and back
            of your hands and keep singing
            your song.
Step 4: Wash in between and all around
            each of your 10 fingers—start
            with your thumb.

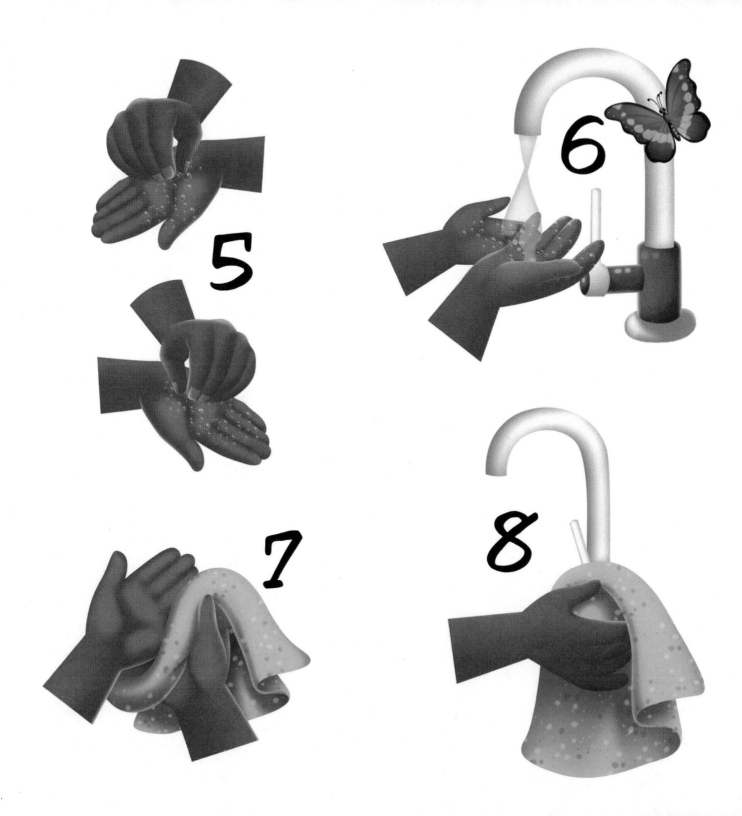

Step 5: Be sure to get underneath your fingernails while finishing up your song.

Step 6: Rinse all the soap off your hands with water.

Step 7: Dry your hands with a towel.

Step 8: Use that towel to turn off the faucet.

The next day at school we learn from
operating room nurse, Mrs. Tish, That washing
our hands to stop spreading germs is her wish.
We can stop people from getting sick,
If you wash those hands really quick.

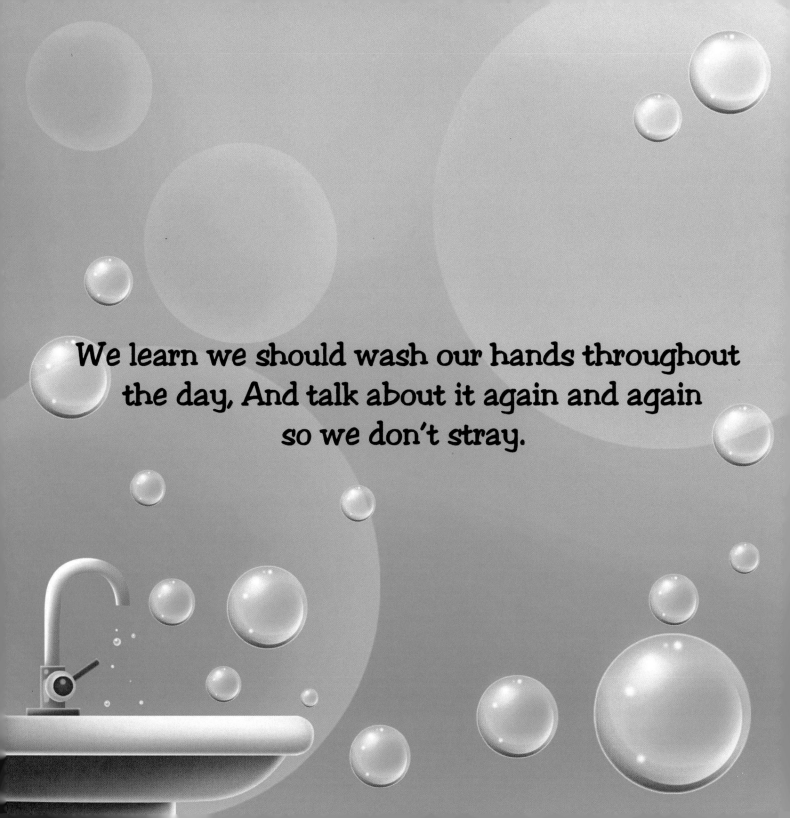

We learn we should wash our hands throughout the day, And talk about it again and again so we don't stray.

We do not touch our nose, mouth, or eyelashes
Because we can spread those germs as quick as light
flashes. Washing our hands keeps others from getting sick.
I will say it again, washing your hands does the trick.

School was over, it was time to go home.
I see Baby Sis and zoom around her like
she is a stone. I have to wash my hands
before a hug and a kiss.

I motion to Baby Sis to come watch my hand washing show, I'm warming up my voice as she arrives at my elbow, I go through the steps to show her how it goes.

1

2

3

4

Step 1: Get your singing voice warmed up "La, La, La."

Step 2: Turn the water on, rinse your hands, and start singing the Happy Birthday song.

Step 3: Rub soap on the front and back of your hands and keep singing your song.

Step 4: Wash in between and all around each of your 10 fingers—start with your thumb.

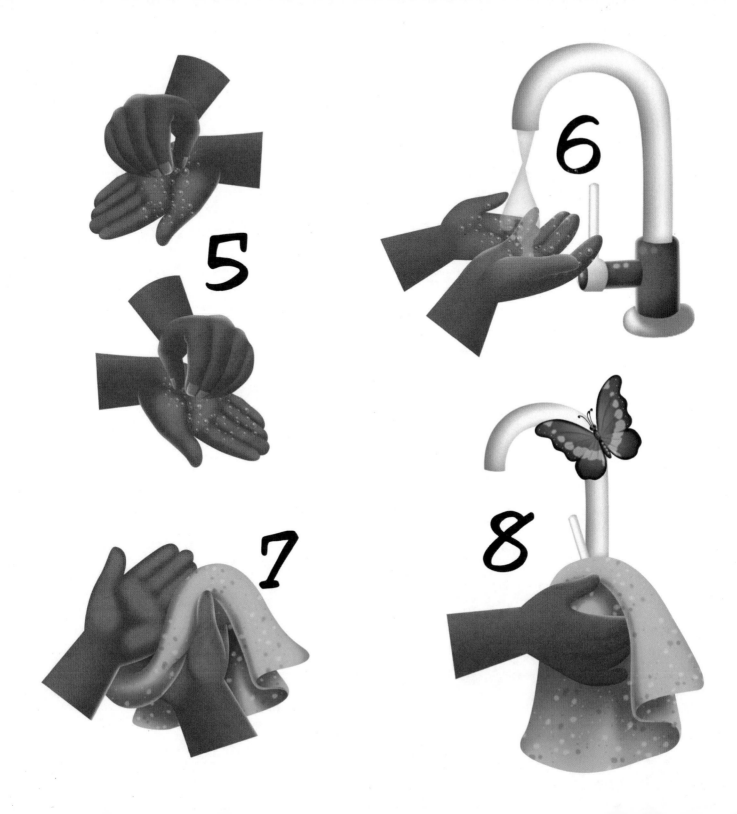

Step 5: Be sure to get underneath your fingernails while finishing up your song.

Step 6: Rinse all the soap off your hands with water.

Step 7: Dry your hands with a towel.

Step 8: Use that towel to turn off the faucet.

Baby Sis smiles and giggles as she is watching all this, I jump down and grab Baby Sis and give her a great big kiss.

Made in the USA
Middletown, DE
15 September 2023

38567133R00022